THERES POWER IN PRAYER

Pastor Mattie Dotson/Marlon l Dotson

Foreword by Marlon L. Dotson

ISBN: 1507555415
ISBN-13: 9781507555415

DEDICATION:

TO ALL OF THE SOULS THAT ARE IN SEARCH OF A HOME IN HEAVEN WITH THE LORD ALMIGHTY, JEHOVA, THE MOST HIGH, AND THE GREAT I AM, THIS IS DEDICATED TO YOU.

CONTENTS

THERE IS POWER IN PRAYER

ACKNOWLEDGMENTS

Prophtess Clarissa Kusi. Prohetess Regina W The Power of Prayer Ministry, Ms Gene Patton, Ms Molly, Victor, David, Sam, Berniece, Rita Grandberry, Bobbie Hill, Martez, Charnelle, Marquita, and Jerome Dotson.

The Power of Prayer

By Pastor M. Dotson

When we pray, what attitude should we have?

We should be both humble and confident. God said, if my people who are called by my name, will humble themselves and pray and seek my face and turn from their wicked ways, then, will I hear from heaven and will forgive their sin and will heal their land. **2 Chronicles 7:14**

Let us then approach the throne of grace with confidence, so that we may receive mercy and find grace to help us in our time or need. **Hebrews 4:16**

What warning did Jesus give us concerning prayer?

We must be careful to not pray in order to be praised by man, and we should not pray with an unforgiving spirit. **Mark 11:25-26**

When you are praying and you remember that you are angry with another person about something, then, forgive him, if you do this, then your father in heaven will also forgive your sin.

Matthew 6:9-13

The Lord prayer is a blueprint for personal living; some people memorize prayer, scripture, but never ever put it into action in their own life. Prayer is communication with God. Worshipping him, praising him, thanking him, and confessing to him. The answer to a prayer depends not upon the will power, zeal, or emotions of the person praying but upon the wisdom and power of God. God looks not for an effort to work up feeling, but for a humble and helpless spirit, that trust entirely in him. Only when believers recognize their helplessness can they really pray in the right spirit, for then they acknowledge that God can do what we can't do. All you have to do is pray with a sincere heart. We can never pray too much if our prayers are honest and sincere. Before you began to pray make sure what you say is sincere. Jesus gave it to his disciples; it can be a pattern for our prayers

Believers pray because they know that God is the source of all good, the controller of all events and the possessor of truly supreme power. By praying they acknowledge that they have no power to bring about the things in which they pray for. But when you pray, go into your room, close the door and pray to your father who is unseen. Then your father who sees what is done behind closed doors, will reward you.

When people pray in the right spirit and with the sincere desire that Gods will be done, they are assured that God will answer their prayers- in so doing he may give something different from what was requested. If believers live righteous and Godly lives they can have confidence that God hears and will answer their prayers. But disobedience, un-confessed sins and unforgiving spirits are hindrances to prayer.

God is all things in life, the good, the bad and in between. Lord, God promises to us-that if we come unto him and pray, he will then give us all the desires of our heart.

John 15:16 - Ye have not chosen me, but I have chosen you, and ordained you, that ye should go and bring forth fruit, and [that] your fruit should remain: that whatsoever ye shall ask of the Father in my name, he may give it you

We have all been pre-approved to receive the desires of our heart. The only thing that we have to do is live, and abide by his word. If you had the winning lottery ticket in your hands, and presently you had no money in your pocket. The first chance you get you are going to make sure you exchange that ticket in for cash. Well, I got news for you good people understanding his word and accepting God as your lord and savior is the lottery ticket of all lottery tickets- not only will he give you wealth, but health, and a sane mind and a happiness that only a Godly person may have.

Do you remember when Hezekiah became deathly sick and Isaiah the prophet went to visit him, he said, Set your affairs in order and prepare to die, Isaiah told him. The Lord say you won't recover. Hezekiah turned his face to the wall. O'Lord he pleaded, remember how I've always tried to obey you and please you in everything I do, then he broke down and cried. So before Isaiah left the courtyard, the Lord spoke to him again. God said, go back to Hezekiah, the leader of my people and tell him that the Lord God of my ancestor David has heard his prayer and seen his tears. I will heal him! He will be out of bed and at the temple. I will add fifteen years to his life and save him. That's just a small example of accepting God and what prayer will do.

THE AWESOME POWER OF PRAYER

."Watch and pray, that ye enter not into temptation: the spirit indeed is willing, but the flesh is weak." (Matthew 26:41)

"When I had fallen to the bottom of the bottom, and my soul and motivations became overcome with despair, and I couldn't find any more strength within myself, I physically gave up and relied on prayer alone. Only then, did I overcome." (Marlon L. Dotson)

WHY IS PRAYER SO IMPORTANT?

Prayer is the natural outcry from the heart of a human being to his Maker in response to the tug of the Word of God, implanted within the conscience.

That tug is even stronger in the heart of one who has had a visitation of the Holy Spirit's convicting presence or has heard the gospel message! The Holy Spirit's call to prayer becomes as natural and desirous as the call for food at mealtime!

"Ask and it shall be given you; seek, and ye shall find; knock, and it shall be opened unto you: For everyone that asketh receiveth; and he that seeketh findeth; and to him that knocked it shall be opened." (Matthew 7:7-8)

When we pray, God not only listens but speaks to our spirits and answers our requests in His own way, according to His divine and gracious will.

The woman with the "issue of blood" touched Him with her faith and received an instant miracle. Jesus turned about in the crowd and asked specifically, "Who touched my clothes"?

Many rubbed shoulders with Him, but one person touched Him by faith. She had said within herself, "If I but touch His garment, I shall be whole." She was made whole, and Jesus declared that her faith had gotten the job done! (Matthew 9:21)

God's Word says: "And it shall come to pass that, before they call, I will answer; and while they are yet speaking, I will hear." (Isaiah 65:24).

'Prayer is talking, listening and communing with God as we enter into the very presence of the Almighty!'

The 20th Century Bible renders the account this way: Jesus said, "Someone has touched me." And they said, "*Master, the multitudes press Thee and crush Thee*". But He answered, "*No, someone has made a demand upon my ability*".

When we believe and reach out for a miracle, we make a demand upon His ability and draw from His great storehouse of blessing, that which we desire! Another beautiful aspect is that the woman received the miracle without Jesus knowing she had a need. The miracle was already accomplished before Jesus was aware of it

GOD MUST COME FIRST IN OUR LIVES

He must take center stage in our lives so that our lifestyle will be pleasing in His sight, and effective in our relationship to others!

Jesus, Who is our grand example, "set His face" to go to Jerusalem where He knew He would die upon a rugged cross and become "a curse for us", in order to purchase our salvation! (Galatians 3:13)

St. Paul said, "*What mean ye to weep and to break mine heart? For I am ready not to be bound only, but also to die at Jerusalem for the Name of the Lord Jesus.*" (Acts 21:13)

Again he stated, "*For I am now ready to be offered, and the time of my departure is at hand. I have fought a good fight, I have finished my course, and I have kept the faith.*" (2 Timothy 4:6,7)

The great apostle was totally dedicated to Jesus Christ. His life was consecrated to His Gospel!

Martin Luther emphasized: "I live as though Jesus Christ was crucified yesterday, arose today & is coming again tomorrow."

The great leader of the Protestant Reformation was consumed with the Gospel of Jesus Christ, and that is why God used him so mightily to bring back the simplicity, truth, purity & power of Christ's Gospel to a corrupt, idolatrous and backslidden Church!

This is the commendation given by the leaders of the Primitive Church regarding the preachers they sent out: "These are men that have hazarded their lives for the name of our Lord Jesus Christ." (Acts 15:26)

Prepare for Battle

No matter where we are at in our lives we will all eventually need to pray. No amount of material or money can change that fact. You will also find that when you began to search for Jesus and ask him to lead you your battles will not be over-as a matter of fact they will have just begun. The *devil* or your *enemy* leaves the un-holy alone simply because their already un-holy, their lifestyle or way of thinking will harm them alone.

There is no need for him to throw a flame on the already burning fire. His objective is to convert those who praise God name and screams halleluiah. So-when your time come to battle the enemy "because that time will surely come "here are some bible verses to help you through. But remember-you must believe!

Prayer without **faith** and **action** is dead.

Proverbs 3:5-6
"Trust in the LORD with all your heart,
and lean not on your own understanding;
in all your ways acknowledge Him,
And He shall direct your paths." (NKJV)

Psalm 46:10 "Be still, and know that I am God: I will be exalted among the heathen, I will be exalted in the earth." (KJV)

Psalm 119:89 For ever, O LORD, thy word is settled in heaven.

Psalm 34:8
O taste and see that the LORD is good: blessed is the man that trusteth in him.

1 Corinthians 13:13 So now faith, hope, and love abide, these three; but the greatest of these is love. (ESV)

John 3:16 "For God so loved the world that he gave his one and only Son, that whoever believes in him shall not perish but have eternal life." (NIV)

Jeremiah 32:27 "Behold, I am the LORD, the God of all flesh; is anything too difficult for Me?" (NASB)

Isaiah 50:10 "Who is among you that fears the LORD, That obeys the voice of His servant, that walks in darkness and has no light? Let him trust in the name of the LORD and rely on his God." (NASB)

Philippians 1:21 For to me to live is Christ, and to die is gain. (KJV)

Matthew 7:7 Ask, and it shall be given you; seek, and ye shall find; knock, and it shall be opened unto you: For every one that asketh receiveth; and he that seeketh findeth; and to him that knocketh it shall be opened.

Psalm 16:8 I have set the LORD always before me: because he is at my right hand, I shall not be moved.

Isaiah 55:12 For ye shall go out with joy, and be led forth with peace: the mountains and the hills shall break forth before you into singing, and all the trees of the field shall clap their hands.

Matthew 6:33 But seek ye first the kingdom of God, and His righteousness; and all these things shall be added unto you.

Psalms 89:1 I will sing of the mercies of the LORD forever: with my mouth will I make known thy faithfulness to all generations.

Romans 8:18 For I reckon that the sufferings of this present time are not worthy to be compared with the glory which shall be revealed in us.

1 Corinthians 15:57-58 "But thanks be to God! He gives us the victory through our Lord Jesus Christ. Therefore, my dear brothers and sisters, stand firm. Let nothing move you. Always give yourselves fully to the work of the Lord, because you know that your labor in the Lord is not in vain." (NIV)

Romans 8:38 – 39 "And I am convinced that nothing can ever separate us from God's love. Neither death nor life, neither angels nor demons, neither our fears for today nor our worries about tomorrow – not even the powers of hell can separate us from God's love. No power in the sky above or in the earth below –

indeed, nothing in all creation will ever be able to separate us from the love of God that is revealed in Christ Jesus our Lord." (NLT)

Galatians 2:20 I am crucified with Christ: nevertheless I live; yet not I, but Christ liveth in me: and the life which I now live in the flesh I live by the faith of the Son of God, who loved me, and gave himself for me.

Psalm 23:4 Yea, though I walk through the valley of the shadow of death, I will fear no evil: for thou art with me; thy rod and thy staff they comfort me.

Isaiah 40:31 But they that wait upon the LORD shall renew their strength; they shall mount up with wings as eagles; they shall run, and not be weary; and they shall walk, and not faint.

Psalm 119:9-11 "How can a young man keep his way pure? By living according to your word. I seek you with all my heart; do not let me stray from your commands. I have hidden your word in my heart that I might not sin against you." (NIV)

Habakkuk 3:19 Although the fig tree shall not blossom, neither shall fruit be in the vines; the labour of the olive shall fail, and the fields shall yield no meat; the flock shall be cut off from the fold, and there shall be no herd in the stalls: Yet I will rejoice in the LORD, I will joy in the God of my salvation. The LORD God is my strength, and he will make my feet like hinds' feet, and he will make me to walk upon mine high places.

Matthew 25:40 "The King will reply, 'I tell you the truth, whatever you did for one of the least of these brothers of mine, you did for me." (NIV)

Joshua 1:9 "Have I not commanded you? Be strong and courageous. Do not be terrified; do not be discouraged, for the LORD your God will be with you wherever you go." (NIV)

Proverbs 1:7 The fear of the LORD is the beginning of knowledge: but fools despise wisdom and instruction.

John 8:32 And ye shall know the truth, and the truth shall make you free.

Psalm 19:14 Let the words of my mouth, and the meditation of my heart, be acceptable in thy sight, O LORD, my strength, and my redeemer.

1 Peter 5:6 Humble yourselves therefore under the mighty hand of God, that he may exalt you in due time.

1 Thessalonians 5:18 In every thing give thanks: for this is the will of God in Christ Jesus concerning you.

Isaiah 12:2 Behold, God is my salvation; I will trust, and not be afraid: for the LORD JEHOVAH is my strength and my song; he also is become my salvation.

Proverbs 28:1 The wicked flee when no man pursueth: but the righteous are bold as a lion

THERES POWER IN PRAYER

The

God within

Most of us are un-aware of the strength that resides in us simply because we do not truly understand God Almighty, *The God Within* and that often leads to us not understanding ourselves completely. In lining yourself up with God and his word, one will definitely have to begin to know themselves, *The God Within*-

For instance, many times in our lives we may keep making the same mistake, not because we want to but because we do not understand ourselves or behavior patterns. We have not taken the time to evaluate ourselves and our behavior, *Self-Mastery*. And in order for one to master themselves they have to understand the Greatness which they are derived from.

When you realize you're the offspring of *Greatness* the God of all Gods you should feel the strength *Within you*. When you realize your father spoke to Moses and told him to tell the Pharoah, *who thought at that time he was the over seer of man*-that he was the Great I Am, and to release his people, you should feel the power of *God Within* you.

The *God Within* is the Jesus in your being!! So, understand and believe that you are a Winner this day. You are a Winner of WEALTH, PEACE, LOVE and Success; Let that be your Mantra not only this day but forever. When you understand his word, and abide by his word, don't be afraid to ask God for the things he said he'll give to you. DEMAND IT!

When you demand it, it shows your faith and belief in the *God Within You* And he doesn't break any of his promises. Anything God promises unlike man-he keeps them all. Your momma, your spouse, may love you, but if you're be around them long enough their sure to come up short every once in a while. But the *God Within You* will not, ever. As long as you serve him, and blesseth his name, and understand that he is your guide, and director, then as long as you believe in him-you and he will become as one, *God Within You.*

You will not truly live and be free until you recognize and accept that Christ lives within you. No man can escape this fact. Without you recognizing the kingdom within you, Diamonds will lose their luster and Gold will seem like wooden sticks, love will feel like and irritable rash upon your heart. But once you accept Christ, *The God Within*, those wooden sticks began to be appreciated for their use of building shelter and the feeling of love starts to shine radiantly on one's heart.

How do we connect to *The God Within* us? We must..

(1)Pray to God and recognize him as our lord and savior.

(2)Meditate and listen for God

(3)Abide by his word

Pray to God and recognize him as our lord and savior.

Count your blessings and be thankful for the good in your life! For God is truly Good, and only good shall come to you today, as long as you recognize that the Lord Almighty, is in control. Behold the Glory of the *God Within.*

I will not cast stones or cast anyone out of the kingdom of God! For I have nor the desire, or the power. All persons, Places, and things are in the father of all creation hands. Understanding, the power of the kingdom within you makes it impossible for you to tear another soul down just to build yours up. Say blessings to the blessed and pray diligently for your blessings while doing so.

Through prayer and meditation God reveals himself, not from the outside but from within you. Although God work miracles on a daily you won't just pray for a car then go outside your house and "Bam" there's a new car. No, Contrary to how many folks, even Christians portray such blessings this is not true.

However, once you've accepted God's word and acknowledge him as the only Lord and Savior he will reveal himself by changing your way of thinking, and filtering all the negative information, and spirits in your life. And only through your faith in him and your devotion to his word will be how you acquire those desires, even the material ones.

For one to talk to the Awake the *God Within* Lord Almighty, he must pray. And for one to listen to him they must meditate.

Meditation is essentially getting rid of all the distractions in your life. If you were to just take notice for a week, of all the things in your life that are distractions, which are those things that interrupt you from hearing God, *The God Within* you may be surprised. A cell-phone, a television, a computer, food, even those people we are around every day. All these things have the potential to cloud your mind with information that has nothing to do with God or your salvation.

I enjoy Gospel music. But honestly, Gospel music alone will not get you closer to God. The only thing that can do that is his word and the understanding of his Word.

On earlier pages I discussed three ways that we can connect with the *God Within*, which is praying, meditating and abiding by his word. These three things are very simple in name but are often hard in doing, but the rewards however are abundant. If you don't believe it, or even if you do, I want you to try it right now and see if the transformation is worth it. Let's start with calling forth to the kingdom and all that he promised to his children. As you read the following words let your heart be consumed with the presence of *The God Within.*

(1) Let Us Pray

“Here I am lord, to all. With the knowing of calling forth your Power of the spoken word. Gen 1;3 The spoken word of God in person Jesus Christ. Let there be light for light is in the spoken word. Here I Am lord. Claiming power over illness, claiming power of my finances, claiming power over wellness. Here I Am lord! Giving up on my thoughts and ideas, and allowing yours to flow through me. Here I Am Lord, claiming power over any bitterness that’s in my heart, any bad wishing to any soul. Here I Am, but a helpless soul who only confides in you understanding that everything on this earth and beyond must consult with you. Here I Am Lord, praising your strength and awakening your kingdom within me, as I flush out the impurities of this world.

I understand that I have Greatness within me, only when I recognize anything and everything that is Great is of you. Here I am! You live in me Lord-so I am of you Lord.

Here I Am claiming power over Disharmony and Doubt. Here I Am, claiming power over flesh filled relationships, that for so long had sucked the life from my spirituality, deferring my journey to you and my salvation. Here I am Lord, changing for the good. Here I Am Lord. Claiming power over my worries that have the potential to cripple my health. Here I AM Lord, reminding you of what you said; you would do for me if only I live by your holy words. Here I Am!!! In your name… I pray, Amen.

Those words to the *God Within* should resonate in your heart and soul. Take a few seconds to absorb the power and feel the slight weight being lifted from your being.

(2) Meditate

After you have let the *God Within* hear you it's time for you to listen. Your answer may not come right then, but it allows your mind to be freed so that when God is ready to answer your prayers-your mind will not be cloudy or contaminated. "The God Within answers all prayers." On a daily basis we probably hear so much negativity that we may not even realize it. There was a saying the older generation would say about bad information: "It goes in one ear and right out the other." This is not true with negativity. The more negative information you hear the harder it is for those positive thoughts to manifest. Negative thoughts sit in your head and produce more negative thoughts, and then those thoughts multiply and that's why meditating is crucial. It rids the mind of negative thoughts, images, and feelings.

Starting with just five-minutes a day, you will be able to keep your one on one line open for the voice and directions of God. This is how we receive our instructions from him regarding what he wants us to do. Meditating is simply connecting to the kingdom within and to everything that is natural on this earth. You'll begin to hear your heart, your mind and not what has been programmed or imputed into you by society. The world and your enemy are unable to decode the messages and plans that God has given to you through meditating. As you start with just five-minutes, monitor the difference in your thoughts, and as they change, increase the time of your meditation. Prayer changes things, and when God answers, it changes our entire being.

(3)Being Obedient

When we begin to walk in the likeness of *The God Within* and waking up the kingdom within us, we become responsible for not only reading and understanding the word, but by aligning ourselves, and behaviors accordingly. Once we recognize the God within, our lives shall never remain the same. It amazes me when I see fellow Christians who go to church like clock-work but yet they find themselves still wrestling with the same exact problem, time after time years later. If you understand and believe firmly in your heart that *The God Within* Lord Almighty is our king and savior, AND YOU ARE OBEDIENT this will not happen. Knowing every scripture in the bible and going to church every Sunday are mere "steps" to becoming one with *The God Within* but your obedience! Is a confirmation of your faith in the word.

No matter how good the sermon is from your Pastor or how much it inspired you, if you are not obedient to the words of *The God Within* that sermon to you was in vein. Only obedience to God's word will bring forth blessings.

What are some things that prevent us from being obedient to God's word?

#1 Until we thoroughly cleanse ourselves the flesh will continue to rule us and the flesh will control the majority of all our activities.

#2 Not understanding the power of *The Greatness within us*.

#3 Associating ourselves with others who do not understand the greatness within them also has the potential to influence us negatively as well. Jesus walked among the unrighteous as well as the righteous but in order for us to do so, our heart has to be completely planted firmly in the word of God in order for us to be strong enough to endure the negative energy from others.

Obedience to God and living an obedient life helps us grow closer to *The Greatness Within.* Obedience in the Christian walk is important so that you can continue to grow and know God's will. Jesus said, that the evidence of a personal relationship with him is doing God's will. "*Not everyone who says to me, 'Lord, Lord, will enter the kingdom of heaven, but only he who does the will of my Father who is in heaven.*'" [Matthew 7:21] Not everyone claiming to be a Christian is truly a Christian. Only those who are in a "*Genuine*" relationship with Christ are the true Christians. Those who know Christ will want to obey him and follow his will. This does not mean that a believer will always do the right things or never sin. It only means that believers have been changed by God's grace and now WALK in relationship with him, following him and living the life that he lived.

Obedience shows our love for God. Christians are not robots, blindly doing what God says without knowing why. We have a love for Christ that so overwhelms that we cannot help but do what he wants. In John 14:21-24, Jesus makes this *connection. "If you love me, you will obey what I command...Whoever has my commands and obey them, he is the one who loves me. He who loves me will be loved by my Father, and I too will love him and show myself to him*"

THERES POWER IN PRAYER

A short story

WHISPER

MARY GREW UP IN HUMBLE BEGINNINGS IN THE INNER CITY. BUT NOW AT THE AGE OF 29 SHE HAD IT ALL, A WONDERFUL CAREER WITH A LUCRATIVE-INCOME. A NICE HOME, A NICE CAR AND A HUSBAND WHO LOVED HER SO DEARLY. ALL THE THINGS THAT THOSE WHO HELPED HER TO GET WHERE SHE WAS AT NOW, NEVER HAD THEMSELVES.

MARY WAS RAISED IN THE CHURCH AND EVERY TUESDAY, WEDENDAY, AND SUNDAY SHE WOULD BE RIGHT UP FRONT WITH HER MOTHER RAIN SLEET OR SNOW. HER MOM PRAYED EVERY DAY TO GOD HOPING THAT HE TOOK CARE OF HER DAUGHTER AS SHE GREW UP AND BLESSED HER, TO BE WHATEVER IT WAS SHE WANTED TO BE IN

LIFE, AND TRUE TO GODS WORD, HE HEARD MARY'S MOM PRAYERS AND BROUGHT IT FORTH TO EXISTANCE.

MARY WAS DOING HER PART ALSO. SHE WOULD STUDY AND STUDY AND WORK DILIGENTLY IN SCHOOL TO MAKE GOOD GRADES. SHE FLEW THROUGH JUNIOR HIGH, AND HIGH SCHOOL WAS A BREEZE. EVEN COLLEGE WAS LIKE KID'S PLAY TO HER. SO-MUCH-SO THAT SHE WAS ABLE TO GET AN INTERNSHIP FROM ONE OF THE NATIONS TOP LAWYER FIRMS DURING HER SOPHMORE YEAR. HER MOMS PRAYERS WERE BEING ANSWERED.

FIVE YEARS AFTERWARDS SHE HAD BECOME A PARTNER AT THAT SAME FIRM AND WAS RANKED AS ONE OF THE HIGHEST PAID IN THE FIRM.

BUT JUST LIKE SO MANY OF US, MARY GOT CAUGHT UP IN HER WORK AND OVER TIME SHE SORT OF FORGOT ABOUT CHURCH. ALTHOUGH SHE WAS ON THE RIGHT TRACK CARREER WISE, HER RELATIONSHIP WITH HER MOM AND FAMILY SUFFERED. HER MOM WOULD CALL HER AROUND THE HOLIDAYS, PRACTICALLY BEGGING MARY TO COME HOME AND SPEND TIME WITH THE FAMILY.

"MOM, YOU KNOW I WOULD LOVE TO COME

AND VISIT, SO I CAN SEE YOU, UNCLE JIM AND THE REST OF THE FAMILY, BUT THEY HAVE ME WORKING ON ONE OF THE BIGGEST CASES EVER NOW." SHE'D SAY TO HER MOTHER.

HER MOM WOULD JUST HOLD THE PHONE AND NOD HER HEAD IN DESPAIR, MENTALLY CALCULATING ALL THE TIMES SHE'S HEARD THIS SAME EXCUSE FROM HER BLESSED DAUGHTER.

"NOW BABY.." HER MOTHER RATIONED WITH MARY WHILE TRYING NOT TO FUSS. "BABY, YOU KNOW GOD GAVE YOU THAT GOOD JOB SO YOU CAN SUPPORT YOUSELF AND YOUR FAMILY, NOT FOR YOU TO DISTANCE YOURSELF FROM HIM OR US."

"OH MOMMA, YOU KNOW I LOVE YALL GUYS. SOON I'LL BE ABLE TO OPEN UP MY OWN PRACTICE AND THEN I'LL HAVE MORE TIME TO SPEND WITH YOU ALL." MARY PROCLAIMED.

"O.K. DARLING."HER MOM SPOKE TRYING TO HIDE HER DISAPPOINTMENT. "I HOPE YOU ATLEAST HAVE BEEN GOING TO SOMEBODY'S CHURCH THEN MARY."

MARY HELD THE PHONE DOWN AWAY FROM HER MOUTH AND MUMBLED IN FRUSTRATION, WHILE ROLLING HER EYES.

"DANG, I WISH SHE WOULD QUIT ASKING ME ABOUT THIS CHURCH MESS, I'M OBVIOUSLY DOING SOMETHING RIGHT, I'M THE HIGHEST PAID AT MY FIRM" MARY UTTERED UNDER HER BREATH, WITH THE PHONE BEING HELD DOWN BESIDE HER LEG GETTING IRRITATED AT HER MOMS TALK ABOUT CHURCH.

"HELLO… MARY." HER MOM RESPONDED TO THE SILENCE THAT LINGERED ON THE PHONE.

"YESSS MOM, IM HERE. BUT I HAVE TO GO . THEY'VE GOT MY DESK SWAMPED WITH ALL THESE FILES, SO ILL CALL YOU BACK LATER-ON IN THE WEEK…OK?"

HER MOM GROANED AND SAID, "OK HONEY, WE LOVE YOU. DON'T WORK TOO HARD."

"I LOVE YALL TO MOMMA." MARY REPLIED DRYLY, WITH NO FEELING AND HUNG UP."

MARY WORKED AND WORKED, PUTTING IN SOMETIMES 17 HOUR DAYS LEAVING HER WITH JUST THE BARE MINIMUM TIME TO SLEEP. EVERY ACCOLADE YOU COULD RECEIVE IN HER FIELD SHE EARNED IT. THE HALF-A-MILLION DOLLAR HOUSE SHE AND HER HUSBAND HAD PURCHASED HAD GOTTEN TOO SMALL SO THEY BEGAN ADDING ON TO IT EVENTHOUGH THEY WERE RARELY THERE TO ENJOY IT.

MARY'S HARD WORK WAS PAYING OFF. SHE HAD SET OUT TO ACCOMPLISH HER GOALS AND GUESS WHAT? SHE ACCOMPLISHED THEM. BUT THE MORE SHE ACCOMPLISHED IN HER CAREER THE FURTHER SHE GOT FROM HER FAMILY AND FROM HER CHURCH. NOT THE CHURCH BUILDING, BUT THE CHURCH IN HER HEART. MARY SUBCONSCIOUSLY BEGAN TO FEEL LIKE SHE COULD DO ANY AND EVERYTHING SHE WANTED TO DO IN LIFE, RATHER IT WAS HER CAREER OR HER PERSONAL LIFE, WITH THE USE OF HER OWN STRENGTH.

BESIDES, SHE HAD GOTTEN THIS FAR WITH JUST HARD WORK ALONE...RIGHT? SHE SLOWLY BEGAN TO FORGET THOSE PRAYERS THAT HER MOM WOULD PRAY FOR HER AT NIGHT. AND HOW HER WHOLE ENTIRE FAMILY WOULD HAVE PARTIES CELEBRATING HER ACHIEVMENTS IN SCHOOL "SUPPORTING HER." THEIR CHURCH WOULD EVEN PUT UP MONEY FOR HER TO GO ON FIELD TRIPS TO WASHINGTON D.C. SINCE HER IMMEDIATE FAMILY WAS UNABLE TO PAY FOR IT BY THEMSELVES.

BUT MARY WAS NO DIFFERENT FROM THE MOST OF US THOUGH. SOME OF US DON'T HAVE GREAT JOBS TO DISTRACT US FROM OUR SAVIOR, BUT SOME OF US HAVE A SPOUSE, OR A FRIEND, A VICE, A

TEMPTATION, OR A DESIRE TO TURN US AROUND AND GET OUR EYES OFF OF THE PRIZE. TEMPORARY HAPPINESS OFTEN TIMES KEEP US AWAY FROM OUR TRUE JOY AND SALVATION.

THREE THANKSGIVINGS, AND CHRISTMAS'S HAD PASSED SINCED MARY HAD LAST SEEN HER MOM AND HER FAMILY DUE TO HER WORK SCHEDULE. AND GUSSED WHAT…MARY OPENED UP HER OWN PRACTICE ALSO.

SO THIS YEAR, MARY WAS ACTUALLY EXCITED THAT THIS YEAR SHE WOULD BE ABLE TO REST A LITTLE AND GET TO GO HOME AND SEE HER FAMILY. SHE HAD HER ASSISTANT TO MAKE RESERVATIONS WITH AMERICAN AIRLINES AND HERTZ RENTAL CAR FOR THANKSGIVING WHICH WAS ONLY A FEW MONTHS AWAY.

BUT ON THAT BRUTALLY COLD, AND CRISP DAY OF NOVEMBER 19TH A WEEK BEFORE MARY WAS TO VISIT HER FAMILY FOR THE FIRST TIME IN A LONG TIME HER MOM HAD PASSED AWAY UNEXPECTEDLY FROM RESPIRATORY FAILURE, DURING HER SLEEP. IT WASN'T REALLY UNEXPECTED, BECAUSE HER MOM AND THE REST OF THE FAMILY KNEW; SHE JUST DIDN'T WANT TO TELL MARY FOR FEAR IT WOULD DISTRACT HER FROM

ACCOMPLISHING HER GOALS, WHICH IN RETURN WOULD PUT HER VISITS BACK HOME EVEN FURTHER ON HOLD.

YOU SEE GOD IS ALWAYS SPEAKING TO US. SOMETIMES HE WHISPERS, AND THEN SOMETIMES HE YELLS. SOMETIMES HE SPEAKS TO US BY LETTING US WORK HARD AND ACCOMPLISHING THOSE THINGS IN OUR LIFE. BUT SO MANY TIMES WHEN WE GET THOSE THINGS WE EITHER WANT MORE OR FORGET HOW HE HAS ALLOWED US TO GET THEM. MARY WAS OVERALL A GOOD PERSON, WHO DONE WHAT MILLIONS OF CHRISTIANS DO. THEY FORGET WHO IS IN CONTROL. THEY FORGET THAT THEY ARE ON GOD'S TIME. CONTRARY TO BELIEF, YOU CAN'T DO ANYTHING ON THE PLANET WITHOUT THE ACCEPTANCE OF JESUS CHRIST IF YOU WANT IT TO BE PROSPEROUS. IF YOU TRY TO DO IT WITHOUT HIM NO MATTER WHAT YOU KNOW OR WHO YOU HAVE BACKING YOU-YOU WILL EVENTUALLY FAIL.

MARY WAS DISTRAUGHT, LIKE ANY CHILD WOULD BE AFTER FINDING OUT THAT THEY HAVE LOST THEIR PARENT. EVEN THOUGH SHE HAD FINANCIALLY DONE WELL FOR HERSELF, HER MONEY COULD NOT GET HER MOTHER BACK, HER MONEY COULD NOT REPLACE THE TIME THAT SHE MISSED OUT ON WHEN HER MOTHER WAS HERE. MARY, WHO THROUGH WORDLY EYES WAS THE SYMBOL

OF SUCCESS COULDN'T ACCEPT THE PASSING OF HER MOM. ALL THE MONEY SHE HAD EARNED, ALL THE TITLES SHE HELD, MEANT NOTHING TO HER AT THAT MOMENT, NEITHER EASED THE ACHE IN HER HEART.

SO ON THAT THANKSGIVING DAY ABOUT A WEEK AFTER HER MOMS PASSING, AND THE DAY OF THE FUNERAL, SHE HAD LISTENED TO THE VOICEMAILS HER MOM HAD LEFT HER, WHEN SHE WOULD PURPOSELY NOT PICK UP THE PHONE-NOT WANTING TO HEAR HER MOM PREACH TO HER ABOUT GOD.

MARY HAD STOOD IN THE COURT ROOM AGAINST MONSTERS AND TYCOONS AND FACED THEM WITH NO FEAR AT ALL AT HER JOB BUT SHE HAD NEVER FELT ANYTHING LIKE THIS-THE GUILT OF NOT LISTENING TO HER MOM WISHES WAS TEARING HER UP INSIDE- SO MUCH THAT SHE SH WENT TO HER MEDICINE CABINET, OPENED UP HER BOTTLES OF PAIN MEDICINE AND SLEEPING PILLS AND SWALLOWED THEM BOTH.

YOU SEE WHEN GOD WAS HELPING MARY GET HER DEGREE; HE WAS WHISPERING TO HER "SEEK MY FACE."

AND WHEN GOD WAS HELPING HER BECOME PARTNER AT HER FIRM, HE WAS WHISPERING TO HER, "SEEK MY FACE."

AND WHEN HE HEPLED HER TO START HER OWN FIRM HE WAS WHISPERING TO HER, "SEEK MY FACE."

BUT MARY COULDN'T HEAR GOD TALKING FOR HER OWN DESIRES, AND THINKING THAT HER ACHIEVEMENTS WERE FROM HER OWN STRENGTH. SO GOD DECIDED TO YELL.

RIGHT NOW AT THIS MOMENT GOD IS WHISPERING TO YOU AS YOU READ THESE WORDS, ARE YOU LISTENING? OR ARE YOU THE TYPE THAT ONLY PAYS ATTENTION WHEN HE SCREAMS. MARY DIDNT LISTEN NOR WAS SHE PREPARED FOR THE SCREAMS OF THE LORD. HIS WHISPERS ARE IN THE FORMS OF GOOD THINGS AND BAD THINGS, AND THE ONLY WAY WE ARE ABLE TO DISTINGUISH THEM IS IF WE, SEEK HIS FACE.

SEEKING GODS FACE WILL NOT PREVENT YOU OR YOUR LOVE ONES FROM PASSING. BUT NOT SEEKING HIS FACE CAN PREVENT YOU FROM HAPPINES AND JOY WHEN THEY ARE GONE AND RECEIVING TRUE SALVATION FOR YOUR LIFE.

(KJ)*Naked I came from my mothers womb, and naked shall I return there. The Lord giveth, and the Lord taketh away; Blessed be the name of the Lord!"*

***Pay attention to the Lord whispers before he yells**

ABOUT THE AUTHORS

PASTOR M.DOTSON

HAS DEDICATED HER LIFE TO SERVE GOD, WITH HER WHOLE HEART. SHE HAS ALSO SERVED AS A FOSTER PARENT FOR OVER TWENTY-FIVE YEARS, PROVIDING A NURTURING ENVIORNMENT FOR NUMEROUS CHILDREN. SHE WAS ALSO CALLED TO MINISTRY IN 1997. ANOTHER IMPORTANT ASPECT OF HER MINISTRY OCCURRED IN 1997 WHEN SHE BECAME THE HOST OF "POWER OF PRAYER TELIVISION BROADCAST ON CHANNEL 19(CATV) ALSO THE POWER OF PRAYER MINISTRY ON 1470 CONTACT; 615/522-1158

MARLON L DOTSON
AUTHOR OF FICTION, NON FICTION, SPIRITUAL, AND SOCIAL LITERATURE.

FOR ANY PRINTED MATERIAL BY MARLON L DOTSON CONTACT (615)638-9876 OR GO TO AMAZON.COM/MARLON L DOTSON.

Made in the USA
Charleston, SC
17 April 2015